I0801768

The INSIDE GUIDE

CELEBRATING HISPANIC CULTURES

Celebrating the People of Mexico

By Rosie Banks

Cavendish Square
New York

Published in 2023 by Cavendish Square Publishing, LLC
29 E. 21st Street New York, NY 10010

Website: cavendishsq.com

Library of Congress Cataloging-in-Publication Data

Names: Banks, Rosie, 1978- author.
Title: Celebrating the people of Mexico / Rosie Banks.
Description: New York : Cavendish Square Publishing, [2023] | Series: The inside guide: celebrating Hispanic cultures | Includes index.
Identifiers: LCCN 2021040428 (print) | LCCN 2021040429 (ebook) | ISBN 9781502664587 (library binding) | ISBN 9781502664563 (paperback) | ISBN 9781502664570 (set) | ISBN 9781502664594 (ebook)
Subjects: LCSH: Mexico–Juvenile literature. | Mexico–Civilization–Juvenile literature.
Classification: LCC F1208.5 .B36 2023 (print) | LCC F1208.5 (ebook) | DDC 972–dc23
LC record available at https://lccn.loc.gov/2021040428
LC ebook record available at https://lccn.loc.gov/2021040429

Editor: Therese Shea
Copyeditor: Jill Keppeler
Designer: Deanna Paternostro

The photographs in this book are used by permission and through the courtesy of: Cover Arman art/Shutterstock.com; p. 4 Subbotina Anna/Shutterstock.com; pp. 6-7 Galyna Andrushko/Shutterstock.com; pp. 9, 29 (center) Diego Grandi/Shutterstock.com; p. 10 Florian Augustin/Shutterstock.com; pp. 10-11 phortun/Shutterstock.com; p. 13 Kobby Dagan/Shutterstock.com; pp. 14-15 Fabio Imhoff/ Shutterstock.com; p. 16 Suriel Ramzal/Shutterstock.com; p. 18 Cezary Wojtkowski/Shutterstock.com; p. 19 Shootdiem/Shutterstock.com; pp. 20-21 achinthamb/Shutterstock.com; p. 22 SL-Photography/Shutterstock.com; p. 25 Dina Julayeva/Shutterstock.com; p. 26 Matt Trommer/Shutterstock.com; p. 28 (flag) J_UK/Shutterstock.com; p. 28 (map) Andrei Minsk/Shutterstock.com; p. 29 (left) CHRISTIAN DE ARAUJO/Shutterstock.com; p. 29 (right) Moab Republic/Shutterstock.com.

CPSIA compliance information: Batch #CSCSQ23: For further information contact Cavendish Square Publishing LLC, New York, New York, at 1-877-980-4450.

Printed in the United States of America

CONTENTS

Different types of wildlife live in the different climates of Mexico. However, pollution and deforestation threaten this land's biodiversity.

Chapter One

WELCOME TO MEXICO

The country of Mexico is officially called the United Mexican States, or in Spanish, Estados Unidos Mexicanos. It lies between the Pacific Ocean and the Gulf of Mexico. It shares borders with the United States to its north and Belize and Guatemala to its south.

Mexico has large mountain ranges, deep valleys, dry deserts, snowcapped volcanoes, steamy rain forests, and beautiful beaches. These environments provide homes for numerous plants and animals. Jaguars, anteaters, spider monkeys, tropical birds, and much more live in the rain forests, while marine creatures such as whales and sea turtles swim along the coasts. More than 100 kinds of cacti grow in the desert.

Natural resources are abundant in Mexico and include oil, silver, copper, gold, and lead. Its greatest resource, however, is its people. Mexico's people mostly live in the center of the country, between the desert of the north and the tropical climate of the south.

Fast Fact

Every year, millions of **migrating** monarch butterflies fly to the mountain valleys of the Mexican state of Michoacán. Their black, orange, and white wings transform the landscape.

Mesoamerican Peoples

The **indigenous** peoples of Mexico likely traveled over a land bridge from Asia and down into North America before settling in Mexico. Over generations, civilizations such as those of the Olmecs, Aztecs, Maya, and Toltecs developed. Though different, they shared practices such as **ritual** sacrifices, study of the stars, and ranked social groups. They built cities and pyramids and learned to shape their world through agriculture, mathematics, art, and religion.

Indigenous **Mesoamerican** peoples, sometimes called Amerindians, often value tradition and speak languages that have been used since **pre-Hispanic** times, before the introduction of the Spanish language. In fact, more than 50 native languages are still spoken by more than 100,000 people in Mexico. Other elements of Mesoamerican arts, **customs**, and history are powerful parts of Mexican identity too.

Diverse Nation

Mexico's Mesoamerican peoples still make up a significant part of the country's **diverse** population. However, some Mexicans are connected more to their Spanish **ancestors**. Spain colonized Mexico for 300 years beginning in 1521. Mexico became an independent country in 1821, though France controlled the nation for a short time in the mid-1800s.

Fast Fact

Mexico is usually labeled a Hispanic country because most of its inhabitants speak Spanish. In fact, it has the world's largest population of Spanish speakers.

The Pyramid of the Sun, in the ancient city of Teotihuacán, is thought to have been constructed about 100 CE. Not much is known about the indigenous people who built it.

HISTORICAL FIGURES

Mexican culture celebrates individuals who have fought for their community. Cuauhtémoc, an Aztec emperor, defended the city of Tenochtitlán from the Spanish conqueror Hernán Cortés in 1521. In 1810, the priest Miguel Hidalgo y Costilla began a rebellion by ringing church bells and calling for a new government. His courage led others to join the movement and the Mexican War of Independence, which ended in a Mexican victory against Spain in 1821. Benito Juárez was a 19th-century president admired for his commitment to improving Mexico. Pancho Villa and Emiliano Zapata were **controversial** revolutionaries who fought for the rights of the poor and Mesoamerican peoples in the early 1900s.

According to an estimate by the U.S. Central Intelligence Agency (CIA), about 7 percent of Mexicans call themselves Amerindians, 21 percent say they are mostly Amerindian, 10 percent say they are mostly European, and 62 percent report they are Amerindian and Spanish.

Fast Fact

Mexico City, the nation's capital, was founded in 1325 CE by the Aztec people of central Mexico. They called it Tenochtitlán.

Today, more than 130 million people live in Mexico, where traditional and modern cultures are colorfully combined and people of all backgrounds come together as Mexicans. Modern Mexico is a blend of many cultures, stories, arts, foods, rituals, and beliefs.

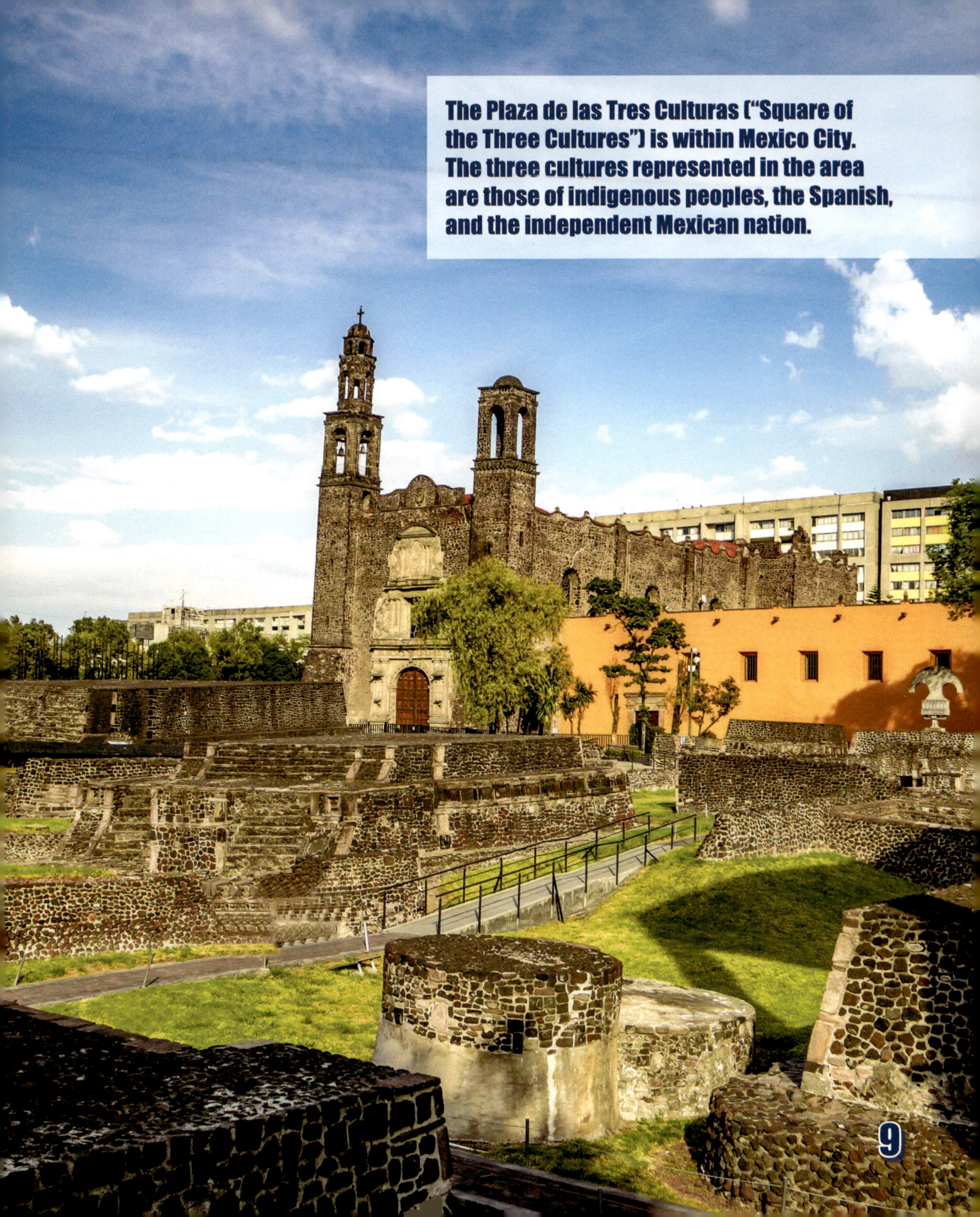

The Plaza de las Tres Culturas ("Square of the Three Cultures") is within Mexico City. The three cultures represented in the area are those of indigenous peoples, the Spanish, and the independent Mexican nation.

Diego Rivera created the *History of Mexico* mural in the National Palace in Mexico City between 1929 and 1935. It depicts Mexico's history to that point.

THE ARTS OF MEXICO

Chapter Two

Mexican art is as varied as its people. However, murals—large wall paintings—are the most familiar Mexican art form to many. Diego Rivera (1886–1957) was one of the country's best-known muralists. His paintings were commissioned for public buildings in the early 1900s in Mexico as well as in the United States. They tell the story of the Mexican people and draw together Mesoamerican and Spanish influences in historical scenes.

Frida Kahlo (1907–1954) remains the most famous Mexican artist in the world. She painted self-portraits that explored her life story and identity as a woman and as a Mexican. Through her later art, she explored her ancestry: the European side and the indigenous side. The bright colors, simple style, and even the clothing she wore were a tribute to Mesoamerican culture.

Fast Fact

In 1925, a young Frida Kahlo was in a terrible bus accident. During her recovery, she taught herself to paint. She later married Diego Rivera.

HANDICRAFTS

Handicrafts and folk art play an important role in the rich variety of Mexican culture. People in different regions of Mexico specialize in crafts and trades such as pottery, weaving, jewelry making, leatherworking, woodworking, and basketry. Many of these crafts are both functional and decorative. For example, artists make beautiful pots that feature bright colors and flower designs. These pots can be used for food and display. Often, handicrafts are taught in schools and showcase the Mexican love of color and respect for tradition. These arts and crafts are called *artesanía* in the kind of Spanish spoken in Mexico.

Mexican Music and Dance

Ancient carvings of cheerful musicians tell us that music has always been important to the peoples of Mexico. Today, Mexican music and dance mix different cultural styles. Many traditional dances across the nation tell stories using energetic rhythms and movements and colorful, eye-catching costumes.

Mariachi, a popular traditional music style, is a symbol of Mexican **heritage**. Mariachi bands often perform in public places. Listeners can dance along and request favorite songs. Musicians wearing festive clothing play guitars, violins, trumpets, and other instruments.

The music and costumes in a traditional dance give clues to where the dance came from. The Danza del Venado, or the Deer Dance, comes from the Yaqui and Mayo peoples and tells a deer hunt tale. La Iguana,

Many Mexican dances tell a story through the dancers' movements. Costumes often vary depending on the region of Mexico.

Fast Fact

During the *jarabe tapatío*, the man's wide hat, called a sombrero, is placed on the ground. After dancing around it, the woman picks up the hat. The dance closes when she holds up the sombrero and both dancers' faces disappear behind it.

a dance from the Mexican state of Guerrero, copies the movements of an iguana. The national dance of Mexico is a couple's dance called the *jarabe tapatío*, sometimes known as the Mexican hat dance.

Mexican Writing

The earliest writings in Mexico used symbols for words and ideas. Ancient people recorded important events by drawing on long, folded sheets of leather, cloth, or paper. Other Mesoamerican stories and poems were told from memory and preserved through storytelling. Many were translated by the Spanish later.

Today, about 98 percent of Mexicans speak Spanish, and most Mexican literature is written in Spanish. For many years, much of Mexican literature centered around the Mexican Revolution. Later, patriotism became a popular theme. One of the most famous Mexican writers is Nobel Prize winner Octavio Paz (1914–1998). He wrote poetry and essays that explored Mexican culture.

Fast Fact

The Mexican Revolution (1910–1920) ended the rule of Porfirio Díaz in Mexico and later established a **constitutional republic.** Among the leaders of the revolution were Emiliano Zapata and Pancho Villa.

An ancient Aztec book is often called a codex. Pre-Hispanic codices used pictures. Later, during colonial times, some showed pictures with words.

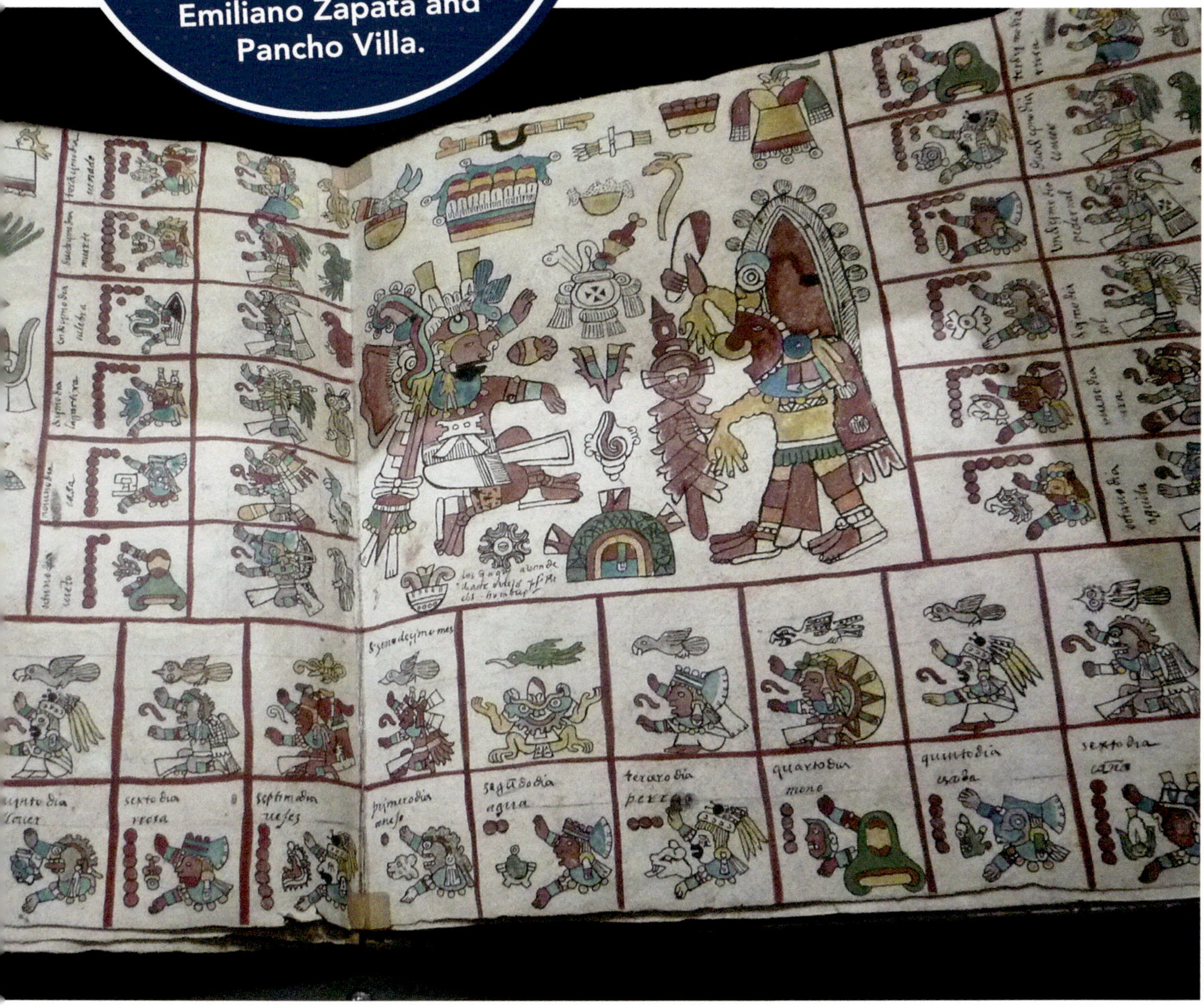

Pan de muerto ("bread of the dead") is a type of sweet roll that Mexicans eat during Day of the Dead celebrations in early November.

HOLIDAYS AND OTHER TRADITIONS

Chapter Three

Mexican holidays are a mix of Catholic holy days, Mesoamerican traditions, and national pride. Family holidays, such as birthdays, are observed with gatherings and meals. National holidays, such as Independence Day (September 16), are celebrated as a community with parades and parties. Religious holidays are celebrated with activities such as going to church.

Mexicans remember and honor their dead. Día de los Muertos, or Day of the Dead, is celebrated each November 1 and 2. A feast of favorite foods is prepared and laid out on an elaborate altar with bright yellow-orange marigolds, photos, gifts, and skulls (*calaveras*) made from sugar. Some families stay overnight in cemeteries. They light candles, sing songs, pray, and eat together as they share memories of their loved ones who have died.

Fast Fact

On May 5, 1862, Mexico defeated the French in a battle celebrated on the holiday Cinco de Mayo. However, France controlled Mexico for several years, withdrawing in 1867.

Traditional Clothing

Most Mexicans today wear modern clothing also found in the United States and many other countries, but some choose to wear traditional clothing for

RELIGION

Religion often influences cultures, including their holidays, traditions, and everyday practices. This is true in Mexico. Pre-Hispanic cultures had their own religions. Though some Mesoamerican religions are still practiced, most are combined with Roman Catholicism. More than 80 percent of Mexicans are Roman Catholic. The story of Juan Diego, the first Catholic saint indigenous to America, is commemorated by Mexicans yearly on December 9. Believers say that Mary, the mother of Jesus Christ, appeared to Diego outside Mexico City in 1531 and asked him to build a church there. She spoke his Mesoamerican language. The church, called the Basilica of Our Lady of Guadalupe, was completed in 1709 and can be seen below.

The backstrap loom, shown here, was used by indigenous peoples in Mexico before Europeans arrived. It's still used by some weavers to make clothing.

celebrations. Others wear it every day. Blouses, wraparound skirts, and shawls are woven from dyed wool and cotton thread and decorated with detailed embroidery. Patterns change from village to village, so people may know where someone is from based on the design of their clothing.

Many women wear a huipil, which is a long tunic with an embroidered design. For festivals in central Mexico, it's common to see the china poblana. This is a style for women that combines a blouse with a full skirt.

The guayabera, a kind of shirt, is worn by men, especially in Yucatán and Veracruz. Men also dress in clothing inspired by charros, or Mexican cowboys, for

Fast Fact

The rebozo is a shawl made of cotton, wool, or silk with different colors and patterns. It can be worn or used to carry goods.

special occasions. They may wear sombreros, fitted jackets, and pants with embroidered designs and shiny buttons.

Ancient and Modern Sports and Games

Sports are part of the Mexican culture too. For thousands of years, Mesoamerican peoples played a certain type of ball game. Two groups competed to get a rubber ball past the other team and into a stone hoop. The players used their hips to pass the ball. The players were often warriors who participated to build their strength. Sometimes, the game was part of a religious ritual. This game is being revived in Mexico today.

Chichén Itzá, an ancient Maya city in Mexico, has the largest ball court discovered to date. The playing surface is 545 feet (166 meters) long and 223 feet (68 m) wide.

Fast Fact

The oldest-known ball court dates back to around 1400 BCE.

The most popular sport today in Mexico is soccer, called *fútbol*. Other Mexican sports include bullfighting and *charreadas*, or rodeos. A style of wrestling called *lucha libre* is popular too. Lucha libre fans fill large arenas to cheer on wrestlers. The wrestlers have practiced the matches beforehand, and they're more like movie or TV characters than athletes. They even wear fancy costumes.

Many Mexican cooks still make their own tortillas, shown here, and serve them hot off the stove. Others use electric tortilla presses.

Chapter Four

BLENDING THE OLD AND NEW

Throughout their history, from pre-Hispanic times to today, the people of Mexico have found creative ways of adapting to life while preserving a **unique** identity. At times when their culture was threatened, Mexicans held onto old customs while accepting new ones, as they did with religion and language—and food.

Cuisine

For some, their first contact with Mexican culture is Mexican food. In many ways, Mexico's food reflects its history. Beans, corn, and chilies have been eaten in Mexico since pre-Hispanic times. Chocolate, potatoes, and tomatoes are also staples of Mesoamerican meals. The Spanish brought livestock as well as dairy products like cheese. They also introduced some herbs and spices, including cilantro and garlic.

Fast Fact

Chocolate was a favorite treat of the Aztecs and is still used in traditional recipes and special sauces.

Today's Mexican cuisine, or style of food, is known for its spicy and flavorful combinations. There are more than 100 kinds of Mexican chilies, or hot peppers. They come in many different shapes, sizes, and degrees of spiciness.

Spices and herbs such as cinnamon, cloves, cumin, thyme, oregano, and cilantro are also used to flavor Mexican dishes. Some more unusual ingredients, such as crickets, insect eggs, and cacti, also shine in traditional Mexican cooking.

Mexican American Culture

The blending of cultures and customs is not new to Mexican Americans. Mexican Americans make up about 11 percent of the U.S. population. They bring with them unique traditions and celebrations. Many Mexican American communities support each other, speak Spanish together, and honor their heritage.

Mexican traditions are seen everywhere in the United States. For example, many Mexican Americans throw quinceañera parties. A quinceañera is the celebration of a girl's 15th birthday. Another example can be found in Brownsville, Texas, near the border of Matamoros, Mexico, where people come together to celebrate Charro Days Fiesta. During this annual event, Mexicans and Mexican Americans share stories about their past and celebrate their identity today. By continuing to practice old rituals and create new traditions, Mexican Americans celebrate their binational culture.

Fast Fact

Mexican Americans make up almost 62 percent of all people of Hispanic heritage in the United States.

Past, Present, Future

Mexico faces challenges today. Its society is marked by a deep divide between rich and poor. However, the nation as a whole wields great power as a key economic and

Día de los Muertos celebrations have become popular in the United States.

The symbol on the Mexican flag comes from a legend. The Aztecs searched for a place to settle marked by an eagle on a cactus eating a snake. They found this sign and built the city of Tenochtitlán, later Mexico City, in the middle of a lake.

WHICH WORD?

Mexico is usually included as part of Latin America. So are the people Hispanic, Latino, or something else? These terms are often confused. "Latino," "Latina," and the **gender-neutral** term "Latinx" describe a person living in the United States whose ancestors are from Latin America, including the country of Brazil (where people speak Portuguese, not Spanish). Mexican Americans might call themselves "Latinos" or "Latinx," while Mexicans might use "Hispanic." Other people don't use any of these terms. It's important to honor the exact language people prefer. It's a sign of respect to ask them if you don't know.

Fast Fact

The Aztecs were also known as the Mexica, which is where the name for the country—and its people—came from.

political force in Latin America. As Mexico faces the future, there will be more opportunities to redefine what it means to be Mexican.

To examine Mexican culture is to appreciate the many ways that life can be lived, understood, and celebrated. Mexican traditions are inspiring, colorful, and sometimes mysterious. Observing them can improve our understanding of what it means to be part of a diverse and constantly changing world.

NEED-TO-KNOW INFO

Kind of Government
federal presidential republic

Population
130,207,371 (estimate, 2021)

Total Area
758,449 square miles (1,964,375 square kilometers)

Capital City
Mexico City (Ciudad de México)

Official Country Name
United Mexican States (Estados Unidos Mexicanos)

Kind of Money
Mexican pesos

Number of States
31

Flag

Location

THINK ABOUT IT!

1. Why do you think Día de los Muertos and other Mexican holidays are becoming more popular in the United States and other nations?
2. Why is it important for Mexicans to remember and honor their indigenous traditions?
3. Why are sports considered an important part of a country's culture?
4. Can you think of a part of Mexican culture that you have encountered in your own life? What is it?

GLOSSARY

ancestor: A family member who lived long before you.

biodiversity: The variety of plants and animals living in an area or habitat.

constitutional republic: A country in which the chief executive, such as a president, and representatives are elected by the people and the laws are recorded in a written constitution.

controversial: Causing arguments.

custom: An action or way of behaving that is traditional among the people in a certain group or place.

diverse: Having many different kinds or varieties.

gender-neutral: Not referring to a specific gender.

heritage: The traditions and beliefs that are part of the history of a group or nation.

indigenous: Having to do with the first peoples of an area.

Mesoamerican: Of or relating to the southern part of North America and Central America that was—at one time—occupied by people with shared cultural features, such as the Maya and Aztecs.

migrate: To move from one place to another as the seasons change.

pre-Hispanic: Of or relating to the cultures in North, Central, and South America before the arrival of the Spanish.

ritual: Having to do with a religious ceremony, especially one consisting of a series of actions performed in a certain order.

unique: Being the only one of its kind.

FIND OUT MORE

Books

Cassriel, Betsy, and Ricardo Mora. *My Teenage Life in Mexico*. Broomall, PA: Mason Crest Publishers, 2018.

Gitlin, Marty. *Mexico*. Minneapolis, MN: Bellwether Media, 2018.

Sheen, Barbara. *Growing Up in Mexico*. San Diego, CA: ReferencePoint Press, 2018.

Websites

Mexico
www.ducksters.com/geography/country/mexico.php
Read this quick-fact overview of the nation's economy, history, and more.

Mexico Facts
www.kids-world-travel-guide.com/mexico-facts.html
Learn more about the unique geography and landmarks of Mexico.

***National Geographic Kids*: Mexico**
kids.nationalgeographic.com/geography/countries/article/mexico
National Geographic Kids has more interesting information about and photographs of Mexico.

Publisher's note to educators and parents: Our editors have carefully reviewed these websites to ensure that they are suitable for students. Many websites change frequently, however, and we cannot guarantee that a site's future contents will continue to meet our high standards of quality and educational value. Be advised that students should be closely supervised whenever they access the internet.

INDEX